the Flicker tree

OTHER BOOKS
BY NANCY HOLMES

—

Open Wide a Wilderness:
Canadian Nature Poems, Editor
(Wilfrid Laurier University Press, 2009)

Mandorla
(Ronsdale Press, 2005)

The Adultery Poems
(Ronsdale Press, 2002)

Down to the Golden Chersonese:
Victorian Lady Travellers
(Sono Nis, 1991)

Valancy and the New World
(Kalamalka Press, 1988)

the ℐ*licker* *tree*

❧ OKANAGAN POEMS

NANCY HOLMES

RONSDALE PRESS

THE FLICKER TREE
Copyright © 2012 Nancy Holmes

RONSDALE PRESS
3350 West 21st Avenue
Vancouver, B.C., Canada V6S 1G7
www.ronsdalepress.com

Typesetting: Julie Cochrane, in New Baskerville 11 pt on 13.5
Cover Design: Julie Cochrane
Paper: Ancient Forest Friendly Silva — 100% post-consumer waste, totally
      chlorine-free and acid-free

Ronsdale Press wishes to thank the following for their support of its publishing program: the Canada Council for the Arts, the Government of Canada through the Canada Book Fund, the British Columbia Arts Council, and the Province of British Columbia through the Book Publishing Tax Credit Program.

Library and Archives Canada Cataloguing in Publication

Holmes, Nancy, 1959–
    The flicker tree: Okanagan poems / Nancy Holmes.

Issued also in electronic formats.
ISBN 978-1-55380-183-2

    1. Okanagan Valley (B.C.: Region) — Poetry. 2. Nature — Poetry.
I. Title.

PS8565.O637F55 2012   C811'.54   C2012-904849-6

At Ronsdale Press we are committed to protecting the environment. To this end we are working with Canopy (formerly Markets Initiative) and printers to phase out our use of paper produced from ancient forests. This book is one step towards that goal.

Printed in Canada by Marquis Book Printing, Quebec, Canada

this book is
for Dave

AUTHOR'S NOTE

—

In a recent talk, Jeannette Armstrong noted that in the Nsyilxcen language, *tmxʷulaxʷ*, the word that is usually translated as *land*, is an amalgam of "time/ living beings/ here (this exact place)" with the concept of "braided" or "spiralling" or "one thing that can be seen as many things (like a braid)." The word for *land*, therefore, might be translated as "this very place in its braided spiral of time and living beings."

CONTENTS

– II –

This Place Here: Okanagan Places and People

– III –

Woodhaven:
A Crisis of Place

SONG AND SUSTENANCE

—

not where fields are pruned into harps
and forks

not between scales
of plate glass and cement

 but in wild spots
 in nests of pine needles

bitterroot opens its pink mouth

– I –

Living Beings:
Okanagan Plants
and Animals

Earth Star

Mushrooming in the fall, in the north part of the valley,
a group of us leaves our cars on a logging road
and delicately tramples the woods. We're not on a hunt
for precious chanterelles or elusive lobsters. Instead
we're collecting specimens to study the world of fungi.

Heads down, rain swept, we gently pry and scoop
the shaggy manes, the slippery jacks, orange
witches' butter, tiplers' bane, Alaskan
gold, cafes of tiny pink cocktail
umbrellas, miniature reefs of creamy coral.

Logged two or three times, the woods are grazed and thin,
wrecked with beautiful litter: lichen-crusted
branches, broken trees, cow patties, muddy
ruts filled with yellow leaves, needles, shredded
pine cones, and electric bolts of larch and cottonwood.

I don't how or when, but I wander away, get lost.
I hear nothing but cawing crows, see no one, nothing
but trenches of tangled logs and unreadable paths
while all around me mushrooms quietly conduct
their chemical experiments on the forest floor.

Then the rain stops. In sunny spokes of light
the forest preens and patters. A nuthatch skips
scritch-scratch dancing down a nearby fir.
No map, no phone, no compass — an orbit of solitude.
In my hand, a cloth bag of mushroom beings.

Soon I find a barbed wire fence, follow
it to a dirt road which leads to a larger road,
where two guys in a truck stop and give me directions
to town. They'll try to find my group and tell them
I am found. Except no one had noticed that I was lost.

Far more lost are the fungi, tumbling onto tables
at the community hall. Damp, trailing moss, our pickings
lie unveiled, dozens of naked, glistening,
amputated, knobby treasures. Gills and pores
are probed and specimens named with book in hand.

Amongst them sits a marvel called the earth star.
Its rind unpeels and opens into the shape of a star
to reveal a globe balanced on that star-skin pedestal.
If you squeeze the ball, puffs of black spores toot out.
In awe, we crowd around this entrancing toy,

in awe at the complexity of life, of nature, revealed
in this one room so far from the *mysterium*
of forest — stunning species, intricate puzzles
of evolution — splayed before us, pierced,
lost again, yet still at home, on this earth star.

Red-Tailed Hawk

for my father, October 11, 2009

The morning of the day you died
a red-tailed hawk launched over
the light-filled valley. All that air,
and you struggled for breath.

New grief is exhausting. All the memories.
It's hard to carry them around
day and night. My dreams
are long and stormy, tears
blot my thought.

From touch to mind,
from then to now, you made me.
From the first track laid in the brain,
to my hand on your stone-like head.

The wildness of a back alley childhood
was rich with your gifts — in summer
raspberries and carrots from gardens you grew,
in fall, shiny as Christmas wrappers,
decapitated mallard heads toppled
by the bloody axe, the feathers, the books,
your stuttering words of love,
the many schools, our arguing
about justice, our restless moving
across country, rivers, lakes and granite.

The morning of the day you died
was the first killing frost,
hunting weather.
In the Arctic blue sky you loved,
the red-tailed hawk circled,
spiralling further and further away,
its tail lustred open
and tendoned like a pale hand.

The hawk will ride the currents
of my memory of this day,
a luminous bird banking in flight,
your bed wheeled out the door,
out of sight for always,
as you sink into what's cold and bitter,
fall into a thought that's air.

The Flicker Tree

Sometimes in the fall
I walk by a ponderosa pine
and glimpse inside
among its sunlit branches
and orange bark
flashes of red, rustling
and pulsing like blood-filled veins
or inner fire.

The tree is filled
with northern flickers
who, in other seasons, are
solitary birds or simply coupled.

Perhaps they gather
in these flaring congregations
for comfort,
wracked by their own autumnal cries
so piercing and sorrowful
that when I hear them
I too am candled
by freshened embers of grief.

Owl in Dust and Ash

in memory of Sylvia Russell

When a bird hits a window,
it sometimes leaves a trace
upon the glass, a bit of down
or gluey speck from a crushed
insect, wet eye, or broken
feather. For days the mark
reminds you of the thud that stopped
you, drew you sick at heart
to the window sill
to see the bird still or stunned
on the patio stone.

The fall my dear friend was dying,
an owl crashed into her bedroom window.
Instead of tuft or smudge, it left
a whole spread-wing powder print
of itself, its coating of summer dust and ash
halo-smashed onto the pane of glass.
For weeks, no rain or weather washed away
that x-ray etching. We watched fall
drop into winter through its transparent
head, body, and cloud-filled wing.
I knew I'd never see the like again,
not she, so looming and vivid in my life,
not an owl clocked
full speed at the moment
between flight and blow.

Snk'lip

The only Okanagan word I recognize
is your name
slinker, road clipper,
poodle eater,
howling away in glee
as I phone the city, the SPCA,
the vet: "What should I do
with this dog leg I found?
The white curly hair's still on it!"
Howling, as I pathetically put it
in the freezer: "Who's missing
their puppy?" As if you care, yip yip yipping
and rolling in the bunch grass, rubbing off
the gold-grey colours,
knocking the grass seeds out of their towers
topsoil flying off like fur in a fight
your jacket now plastered
with billboard bling, loving it
strutting around with garish ad jewellery
golf, lingerie, hamburgers, dentists, condos
sunglasses the size of swimming pools
hanging onto your real estate buddies
Stoehler, Swindell, and Profit,
panting on their leashes, leashes
the size of bulldozers
kicking out those homeless
snakes, owls, pine trees
and other weaklings.
You love the greed, the gas,
who wants a story if you can get a deal?
Rip up the place!
Rip! Rip! Rip!

You'll be the new road,
the gravel pit, the Hummer, the toothy
subdivision with the maniacal grin
crawling up the hillside
pulling your magic shit behind you,
your RVs, your boats, your garbage cans, your sprinklers,
waving down at the appalled lake.
Hey! you teeter on the dynamite,
Look at how high I can go!

                              Look at me!

Finch Feeder

I am a dealer.
The junkies sit all day
at the dangling syringe,
shooting up black seed.

In my backyard,
it's opiate, sleepwalkers, pine needles,
dopey heat, and sometimes
murderous owls, but still
the addicts
shove each other off
the stools to get to the bottle.

Goldfinches hallucinate. Siskins,
high and crazy,
crack my windows. House
finches, cling to perches,
housewife habitués,
aprons still stained
with raspberry preserves.

But I'm a dealer,
so nothing —
no broken home,
no mental case —
nothing
will stop me pushing.

Mourning Dove

When it lifts itself into air,
it creaks like a squeaking wheel,
a steam-punk flying machine,
goggle-hatted,
a Chitty Chitty Bang Bang,
every crunchy seed and insect in its belly
grated into fuel
for the aching, groaning, gravity
dragging act of flight.

Settled aloft,
it coos gloomily
why do this? why do this?
up in the pine's soft claws.

Saskatoons

zither shins,
stringy bloom bows, bees
revving in sawtooth leaves, roots
cackling in hot gravel, spiky
punk head berries blacken
dark as bear fur, we crunch
seedy beach sand in teeth
till fall raisins them, yellows and thins
twigs into paupers, slum brush, rusted out
cars, flaking paint,
scraps dished out to every
swiping hand, beak, paw

so unlike the plush peach orchards:
fleshy thumbs sorting and stacking
shade and leaves, and fat-ass fruit
piling up in bank accounts

Logs

in winter
mountains disembowel
the clouds

logging trucks rumble
through each town with boxcar loads

each tree leaving home
carrying its whole life
rolled up inside it
like a carpet

California Quail

They land in deep snow:
a flop of flight,
a puff,
and then they disappear.

Until you notice
they are strutting around
submerged,
and, poking above the snow,
their antennae feathers

wag along
like finger puppets
escaped
from the kids' Christmas stockings.

Swans in January

What I like about January
is that swans come to the lake.

For a week or two, they borrow a bay.
Their necks ballet

pure muscle and bridal satin, their black glove
beaks bow to the ice-rimmed beach,

tucking, preening, turning,
slowly spilling open
in a lake-lens time-lapse camera.

Watching them, I dream my most naked
winter thoughts

and when they fly away
I'm with the lake

as it lifts a wet and silver eye
along their northbound flight.

What a dead undecorated winter,
the year they do not come.

I grow cold and shabby,
turn against my blankets, my winter clothes,
turn against the lake.

                              I cannot
comb its icy locks and shores.
I will not.

Sagebrush Buttercup

March 2nd. The western side
of Giant's Head Mountain

is a fossilized stone engine
corrugated with columnar jointing,
volcanic pistons millions of years old,
rusted solid, shut down.

But today
the derelict stone suddenly erupts
with buttercups,

the newest things on earth —
open innovations.

Let's push these yellow buttons
and start the spring.

Sagebrush Mariposa Lily

When I see it in early summer
rising like a fantasy out of last year's
grass, I feel my own flesh
unpeel from the stem of my bone,
become petalled,
muscle and skin
thinly scalpeled open, purple,
bruising, incarnate
in wind and sun.

Yellow Bell

it's spring truly

garage sales sprout up everywhere
never mind the rain
squalls and sunny speeding cloud

today we're going to sell
that one yellow dress
on the mountain, dangling
on its hanger

blowing open
          bell-like
in the wind

Magpie

Flutter-leaping from tree to tree, tail
clicking, those swinging walking sticks, the magpie's
leading me down the trail
to where the lake is lit up
so spiritually.

I turn around and see another magpie
dive-bombing my dog's head.
Rat-a-tat,
      rat-a-tat,
            rat-a-tat-tat-tat.

As usual, I've been led astray.

Arrow-Leaved Balsamroot

April

when muddy sky
erupts
with big patches of yellow
     so do the Okanagan hills

       the sky's outbreak
            and the hills' too
        of sun
     flowers

August

scabby slopes
could flare up any time
     with lightning

crusted hills
dull
     scratched by pine needle

rash days gone now, though seed
itches in its cradle

memory seals its salve
     finds shade

Blazing Star

in the rubble at the foot of the cliff
next to the old volcano gone
bankrupt and stone cold
dead, at the edge
of the junkyard, it set up camp
with its roll of barbed
wire, its olive grey uniform

there   crouched
in the dirt, behind
a broken rock
bristling with weapons
and thorns
it waits all winter, through
fitful spring

by summer, so hot and
jittery that by accident
a golden rocket explodes
        gravel spits underfoot
and you go down seeing
the long shooting eyelashes   and bony wrists
of the boy soldier
who doesn't know
the war is over and they have lost
the planet,
everything

Bluebunch Wheatgrass

for Don Gayton

Sitting by a tuft of bluebunch wheatgrass,
after Don has formally introduced us,
I think how a name is a door.

Amongst the meadowy crowd
of sand, spider, scrub, and sage,
I now recognize this grass
and knock on its door, be friendly, distinguish it
from its tufty company.
Bluebunch wheatgrass,
its crooked stalky smile and dusty skin,
will surely open up, invite me into
its kitchen.

Unless it suspects me of being
yet another salesperson, utopian,
hell spinner, cattle trampler, lawn grower,
chemical leaker, machine pusher, seed sinner,
sitting at its table
while making a pitch and planning
its eviction.

I think of the photo of the man holding in his arms
an uprooted plant of bluebunch wheatgrass,
its long-hair draped over one arm,
feverish with erosion,
while the rest of its dirt-filled body
of roots, heavy as the pelt
of a large mammal,
drags
its corpsy feet
on the ground.

Butterflies

for Dennis St. John

Next to the new power station,
where the antelope brush has been ripped out,

the butterfly hunter raises his net.

Sun fuels the butterflies' flight
       and they toothlessly,

               weightlessly,
flaunt

their eyelid-tugging,
         solar-sallying

helplessness.

Toads Are Us

I just read this:
"The planet's health can be measured
by the state of its amphibians."

So, I am proud of the toad in my garden.
My grass and dew are clean.
My shade is certified organic.
The dandelions in the lawn
sing like canaries
in their light green cages.

But toad,
I watch you cling to the lip
of my flowerpot,
and feel a little worried.

You are
trembling and
you look like a piece of my lung
torn out.

Watching the Coopers' Hawk Nest

for Lori Mairs

One Nikon D3100 digital SLR with zoom lens,
one HD Sony video camera,
one Bushnell Legend Ultra-HD birding scope,
and two decent pairs
of high-power binoculars,
a pot of coffee on the stove,
and we're ready for surveillance
of this family of terrorists.

Swallowtail Butterfly

There are dark rumours about her past.

When young, she was a cripple,
      disabled by a giant pair of wings
            like crushed umbrellas
                  inside her body.

Then she had the operation,

the dermaplaning of fat and tissue,
      excisions and suctions,
            the snapping and re-doing of head and jaw.

From the charnel house,
from plastic surgery and chronic pain,
           this golden summer stunner comes.

Her sifty yellow fans seduce me,
      her dresses track the sun
           in sexy lace.
Lazuli this and blonde that.

I follow her round the garden
      with a camera.
           Who cares where she came from,
what she once was.

You may have your monarchs,
      but she is *my* celebrity,
         my Hollywood,

and I'm her paparazzi,
      smitten.

Prickly Pears

like puppies they jump onto the path
where you are walking

they bite your ankles and shoelaces
with sharp annoying teeth
and miniature snarls

you can't kick them off
that's part of the game

you can't pry them off
they nip your fingers

so steel yourself

you've got to take a stick to them
it is the only way

Black Bear

Black bear, there you go again:
walking away.
It's never your fault, is it?
No, I'm always the one making a fuss.
You think it's my hormones,
my psychological difficulties.
Do you know how irritating that is?
As if we don't have a problem.
Your crashing over my fence in the middle of the night
to smash my bird feeders.
Who did that, eh?
Or hanging out in a tree by the path
scaring the shit out of all the neighbours?
Is that well-adjusted behaviour?
Is that my fault?
And it really was you who hit my car,
not the other way around.
I was driving down the road
and out of the corner of my eye
saw a big lumbering dolt and WHAM
you ran into the side of my car!
The wheel rim still has the dent
of your front tooth.
So what the hell
was *that* about?
Could you just stop and listen for once?
Would you stop turning your back on me?
Come on, black bear,
we need to talk.

Snow Buckwheat

tiny paddles of leaves
aluminumed in dust

stemmy joints exposed and
tubes of plumbing

a machine abandoned in the desert

but the orange moon of August
draws from this silver factory
our furthest thoughts

pipes spume
frothy blooms   petalling smoke

manufacturing dreams
of snow and damp
December

Brown Squirrel

I don't know why I don't write a poem
about the chickadee,
my favourite bird, the one I talk to
and whistle at all spring and summer.
It arrows back and forth, back and forth
at my bird feeder all year round
as I shovel snow, rake leaves, or garden.
Black-haired, wheezy, buffy, busy,
upside down, it grows a new brain cell
to remember each seed it secrets away,
our brainiest of little birds.
"The chickadee we have always with us,"
said John Burroughs, and aren't we lucky?
Unlike the brown squirrel, not so lucky,
being driven out by gangs of blacks and greys
from the coast. Glittering like mirror sunglasses,
like silver sports cars, they shake down
whole trees, set off sirens and alarms,
tear down police tape strung
from pole to branch to wire to path to bench
to bush. Hey, bitch, don't tell me
to turn my music down.

I don't know why I don't write a poem
about the chickadee.

Behr's Hairstreak: Capture and Release

"In cadence, each thing declares not only what it is,
nor even how it is — but that it is. At all."
        Dennis Lee, "Cadence, Country, Silence"

early March,
        the desert's sage seedlings
pump their tiny sacs of scent
into the air

somewhere out there — transparent butterfly eggs

        but who knows where and
who can see
the black pea-like embryos inside?

sagebrush buttercups
unbutton
the hill's winter coat

        —

rosy-red ponderosa pine
smells like vanilla when you scratch it
your weak fingernail against that
        armour-thick bark
                with cracks like desert canyons,
like dinosaur scales,
yet
        it is dying of a thousand pinholes
a million million beetles
eating a whole forest

through that thick bark

—

Hummingbirds are back
cavorting with plastic

tubes

dangling on porches
of new stucco houses.

Spring so late this year.
Dry.
So early last year.
Has there ever been an ordinary spring?

Is it enough to have only seventy or eighty
in a lifetime?

What if you have just one?

Is something happening
to earth's equinoctial tilt?

—

"Hairstreaks (subfamily *Theclinae*) are mainly small butterflies,
many with threadlike tails on the hindwing. They fly rapidly,
flitting from side to side or in circles, with movements that
are difficult for human eyes to follow. Most (except for the
scrub- hairstreaks and a few others) perch with wings closed,
revealing the upper surface only in flight. Males of many have
an oval black stigma on the forewing."
— *Kaufman Focus Guide to Butterflies of North America*

in the Okanagan
Behr's hairstreaks are endangered butterflies
they have an evil
black stigma on the forewing

but who sees them anyway?
with their invisible habits

they won't be missed
they're small as a thumbnail,
thin, freckled

they get one spring and
one summer

when they fly
the little sinners
the human eye just won't
keep up

—

their caterpillars
are birdbread
green worms, mmmm

caterpillars so picky
they eat only the leaves
of seventy-year-old antelope brush

most of it mangled by tractors
and bulldozers
so what, kick a few puny worms out
of the folds of bitter bark

come on, hairstreaks:
you had to adapt to find this niche
so get adapting,
you don't have a few hundred years

—

"Plan Ahead,"
says the church sign in Oliver.
"It wasn't raining when Noah built the ark."

So the mathematician and the biologist assemble
their tools:
    – the students
    – the butterfly nets
    – the pens
    – the grant money
    – the GPS systems
    – the Beowulf cluster

the biologist broods about how to carry
test tubes in the desert
so they won't
break
                in backpacks   so the heat
     won't boil
the DNA

—

      in May the streams
are foamy, coppery

     purring water's
what our bodies sound
like from inside

what a baby hears in the womb

the soundscape cancer lives
in its house of bone and cushy organs

the sound of bathwater, wash water, toilet water,
    shower water,
running through ten thousand houses in the desert

so consoling, so refreshing
even when bleach, pharmaceuticals, and chemo start
    to run

—

bulrushes   brown and velvety
like newborn foals

but when you touch them —
stiff upholstery
like your grandmother's chair

let's just stay here, stop moving,
avoid invasive highways, invasive concrete, invasive furnaces
invasive power plants, invasive fences, invasive street lights,
invasive asphalt, invasive fish, invasive purple loosestrife
    choking the crap out of the bulrushes

some like flashy loosestrife with its purple wig
its loud voice,   others want

things that are warm brown and thistly
whistles, red-petalled wings, prickles

here in the ditch we
love the bog, to be bogged
      down

so don't follow the lightfooted loosestrife
over the desert's body

don't vagabond after the vulgar weed

Keep to marked trails.
Be considerate of wildlife.
Take only the right souvenirs.
Report environmental abuse.

Loosestrife, you've been reported
but still your gorgeous garbage
is all over the bank

—

the month of June speaks from the calendar

"I line up each day in neat rows (it starts like graph paper)

inside me the moon waxes and
withers like a growth (quadratic equation)

when it's thin, it's like a cramp
rolling through me (the calculus)

when fat, it stirs a bowl of stars,
makes milky diffusion (the butterfly effect)

but no matter, I line up each day
in neat rows (we call this accounting and not mathematics)

I turn and blacken the moon through my body
one day, one cell, at a time (Fibonacci,
arithmetic, the first prime number)"

—

June is the month when yarrow sets its creamy plates
on the table of the desert

this is the month of the Behr's hairstreak
its little orange lights
skirting the power plants
dipping over gravel pits
flickering through highway corridors
looking for the wiry arms of the antelope brush

mathematics follows them
into the desert,
                    lattice graphs
become a butterfly net
            in this dimension

they are outside language, closer
to mathematics
they trail veils
of equation

Maxwell's equation
diffusion

the bone of the desert is eaten
by sun

—

wires float and zing, cast back
in blue bowl, cross and cast back and up
but not so up in metal strings
air slosh, trampoline down
to carouselling flower
white dancefloor, dancefeet and body prickled
by flower hair,
flung, do-si-does, up on a bounce of wind
feet sticky, wires
zip and sing, stinking block of concrete,
axleing around,
sage scent drinking, ah
acey duecy, wing cartwheel
down, up white wall, boobiddy, boobiddy, white floor, succulent
sashay, diamond, chain and roll,
power plant bows and fiddles
its sad sad song

through the butterfly net's little jacket

fingers pinch a wing
this petal has a mind of its own
sshhh, Female Number 98

GPS coordinates

felt pen dabs
dots onto a wing

a massage, then small messenger of its species
released into a field of yarrow and light

another capture, the net's neat little straitjacket
Male Number 10
900 meters from his first release

GPS coordinates

release into yarrow, pine and sun

capture, release
capture, release

soon the valley is full of graffitied wings

—

I am a blind butterfly hunter
I don't even see
butterflies touch my hair and shoulders

I'm as blind as I am every day
but now I know I'm blind

blind to the brown and orange blinks in grasses
blind to the speckled dance in pine needles
my net is empty

and I am invisible to them
boulder of flesh to bounce over

I blunder on, noticing nothing

but prickly pears!
little surprises!
what are you doing
growing in Canada?

—

always bring your mind back to the bushes,
watch for yarrow, the butterflies' favourite nectar,
distinguish hoppers from true butterflies,
look for a flash of orange,
watch out for prickly pear and that spear grass
which threads through your every net,
every neuron of your mind
must concentrate, must remain aware

and like your mind
the power of their wings
        is a true power

—

the biologist clips
        tiny fragments
of wing
to collect
            DNA

he stores the flakes
        in test tubes
propped in a carved
            potato

a fleshy *trembleuse*

—

hot meadows are batteries,
they charge the butterflies

students stop for lunch
at the foot of pine trees
beetle-burnt and fire-blackened

in the clear arm of the test tube
the bracelet of DNA dangles
its lucky charms

—

within a fifty-metre radius of this poem
someone is trembling at the thought of an equation

possibly not averse to poetry,
this person is panicked at a hint of mathematics

right now, now that I've mentioned it,
the x's and y's and especially the n's
fill this person with anxiety

when the mathematician shows a Patlak model
the room slowly empties

I go home
my thoughts like a bad dog
wondering why I run off
why I won't stay put

—

if the butterflies disappear from the valley
if the antelope brush is pulled from the ground
if the yarrow is dug up with machines
if mathematics turns its face from the earth
if poetry raises its eyes to a sunset
if the earth grows cement-hearted
if the test tubes are filled with grave dirt
if June disappears
if I live in a desert
if the seasons are clogged with low cloud and numbness
if you're blind to the butterfly in front of you

if the butterfly is only a symbol to you
if you want to name your winery or your subdivision after it
if you have multiplication problems
if butterflies don't diffuse like heat because they have minds
                                         of their own

if they fly randomly but with persistence
what can you do for them, the little buggers?
what can they do for you?

     —

a butterfly rests a moment
        on my finger

its legs are threads of flesh
        against my flesh

For several years in the Okanagan, biologists and mathematicians
conducted field studies which marked and recaptured butterflies
(including the Behr's hairstreak) to collect mathematical data
to develop population dispersal models. The goal is to help
conservationists in their work to ensure the sustainability of
butterfly populations in this region that is under intense urban
and agricultural development.

– II –

This Place Here:
Okanagan Places
and People

Cliff

I love to live below a cliff.
Some, I know, prefer the top
and there the view is lovely, but
down here the gap comes to a stop.

From here no one will ever fall
and each is sheltered, one and all,
except the vole who's snatched away
by the plunging bird of prey.

The Spirit of Resistance

You have come to class through the cold
air that wants to get under your clothes
but you won't let it.
You walk into a room so still and dead
even the dry leaf your foot broke on the sidewalk
has more life in it.
In this room, you have no relations.
Here the air loves nothing, not even the virus
that comes out of your lung with a gun.
Each thing in the room is glossed
in plastic or chemical, your feet and elbows
rest on coffin lids of fabric and fossil
boiled and remoleculed.
Your river pebble eyes open
onto chlorine swimming pools.
No sunlight swims here
untubed and unprocessed.
Your cells are not hooks catching the fish of the sun.
Your cells stink in their bags. Time has stopped
washing through your body, rinsing your blades and barbs.
Wildness has been combed out of your tongue.
Your ears are full of machines digging trenches.
Your heart, a frog's deflated belly.
You have no relations. The other beings in the room
are like you, ghosts searching for other ghost faces,
but the rich cloud and compost hair of the underworld
is glued up, cemented over.
You cannot tell if the man in front of the class
is a TV or not. You drift in and out of the room
to turn him off and on.

Once you had a dream that someone
brought a hawk with yellow eyes into this room.
Not an electric dream, but a bone dream.
Backlit wings of a red-tailed hawk pressed into a strong wind
etched a fan shape in your brain.
You dreamt a witness
had come into the room
to testify that you were still something,
that touch had its warm knots in you.

Brown's Creek Blockade
Solidarity Poem

*in support of the Okanagan Nation's protest
over Tolko Industries' plan to clear-cut 27,000
hectares of forest in a community watershed*

Who's disturbing the creek?
Tolko? Is it you, Tolko?
Isn't the creek disturbed enough?
Isn't the snow pack's pressure
so deliriously light
the poor creek is wringing itself dry
day and night?
Isn't the creek having nightmares of landslides,
logging roads, mud, silt, floods, and erosion?
And hot X-ray summers?
The creek is disturbed, Tolko.
Its drainage is ulcerated.
Its melt is runny.
Its channel morphology is off the charts.
The creek is worried about running into a disturbed lake.
The creek is disturbed that
the Crown has no treaty nor bill of sale
to show how it bought the creek.
The creek is disturbed by Tree Farm License 49
and other shady deals.
"We're forecasting the mill to be short of fibre,"
says Tolko.
The creek is disturbed by this talk —
your terrible language, Tolko,
and your other machines.
You're robbing the banks, Tolko.
The BC Supreme Court is warming up your get-away car.

The creek knows it will be
stripped, burgled, raped into a wreck,
left to fry, burn, boil, and spew.
Don't you think you should worry
if your drinking water's disturbed, Tolko?
Tell us, Tolko,
with all that wood you've stolen,
are you planning to build us an ark?

Life Support

How does the moon love the lake?

Like an heirloom, a silver spoon or platter.
It polishes the lake all night
then puts it away.

How does the cloud love the lake?

When it's black
and the lake is bruised all over,
they cry together in sympathy.

How does the valley love the lake?

Like a limb or a tongue,
as the muscle that moves it
and lets it speak.

How does the swan love the lake?

As it is loved.
The lake's white wings
pull the swan out of the air.
They stare into each other's eyes for hours.

Like an eye, *says the blind hill.*

Like a chamber of the heart, *says the stream.*

What lake, *asks the salmon?*

How does the city love the lake?

Like an organ transplant.
The city treats it tenderly,
keeping it warm,
keeping the lake attached to its body
with a thousand tubes,
letting drugs and chemicals
bathe it,
regulating its flow.

The city's reflections
pass through the lake, a kidney.

Cut Off

A poet said the old names of this place
And, as if I had a stroke, I lost my language.
The golden slopes had slipped their leash, escaped
from rootless English, bearing true names which,
wordless, I could no more speak nor read
than clouds' rippling script across the grass.
I live on ancient land, foreign instead
of home.

Harry Robinson

crooked trails, crooked salmon jaws
crooked mountain silhouettes
dapply pebbles in the creeks
dapply cottonwoods along the creeks
magic chalky circles in Spotted Lake
magic chalky necklace in Robert Lake
his eye-blinks jump the fences
his eye burns through No Trespassing signs
his mouth eats property laws for breakfast
his mouth harps barbed wire and power lines
so the web of valleys,
Okanagan, Kettle, Similkameen, Shuswap, Nicola,
zings and sizzles   strings of his stories
puppet dance the farms and towns till they drop
exhausted onto their bed of strip malls

should we follow him, tripping, stumbling,
down the Similkameen, last undammed river
scything banks of silver stone
folded golden hills, steep mountains

but where is he now?

a pair of old shoes laced together
slung over a telephone wire

Giant's Head Mountain Ghazal

Two bears in the backyard, like arthritic acrobats,
fall off the fence and crush the garbage can.

A boulder broke off the mountain.
Now a petrified heart, split in two, lies in centuries of grass.

Machines and houses are crawling into the woods.
Bears take their morning walks earlier and earlier.

"There is no bed yet," the nurse said. "Not until someone's
          sent home
or passes away. Believe me, we're working on it."

Bear scat on the path:
jammy, bony cherry pits.

Black and white, black and white, black
and white. The magpies write notes all over the mountain.

Desert Lawn

flaxy sand   gritty sun
ant-peppered dry tufts   who'd closely
mow this baked grained   who'd lawn it, linen print
all over

whose burnt glade is this meadow
taken   apart   whose brittle
gold razed hill   where?

Grassland Equations

The sun writes its earthly equations in grass.

Grass is the earth's notation of the effect of sunlight.

Winter grass is evidence of the sun's existence beyond the cloud.

Light and grass are earth's envelope, entwined as mathematical theorems with each other and with physics.

The physicist thinks in grass; the mathematician thinks in sunlight.

The poet ties a blade of grass to an equation with a love knot.

The earth is lit up in grass, the universe in mathematical equations.

Grass at my feet, sunlight on my skin, I walk through several laws of physics, love, and mathematics.

Like those higher dimensions, grass is invisible to many unless it's 3-D green.

Only the most lucid and capacious mind is mathematical or recognizes all eighty species of grass found in the Okanagan.

Scars. Ruts. Fences. Woven through the mental slats of sun and grass.

The More We Travel

to Calgary, one hour gone
to Toronto, three hours disappeared
to Paris, eight or nine, I already forget

do we regain them
when we claw our way back
across Earth's huge relentless ball?
no, it's the obliteration
the tiny blanks that last

this travel doesn't take us down paths
of changing forest and fleeing animals,
or weeks of storm and calm,
but cuts out bits of our lives
in surgical meridian chunks

so that they're gone

gone, not like sleep-gone,
full of busy dreams and repairs
not like infancy
when the body *is* the ticking clock,

but rubbed out entirely,
never to be used

so the more we travel away
the more our lives
are full
of little holes

I Wish I Were

picturesque as a hitchhiker poised at a panoramic view
foolish as a hitchhiker dressed in a strapless top and tiny skirt
hopeless as a hitchhiker outside a gated community
sassy as a hitchhiker who bows and waves beside the road
grateful as a hitchhiker in July with a floppy hat and a bottle
     of water
careful as a hitchhiker miles from the next provincial park,
     and that water bottle nearly empty
thoughtful as a hitchhiker dreadlocked in a right-wing valley,
     knowing there's an organic garlic farm nearby
cosmic as a hitchhiker on a logging road where no car has
     driven for days when a stuffed Volkswagen Beetle pulls
     up and offers a lift
resigned as a hitchhiker in a rainstorm
uncertain as a hitchhiker walking towards a car with tinted
     windows
joyful as a hitchhiker who gets a ride in a battered old station
     wagon with a pile of cheery Okanagan guys who don't
     care where they are going

could I not be
so unplanned and undeserving, so slow and setback,
played upon, skeptical, baked, shunted,
passed over, picked
both up and apart?

I could not, it seems,
as I press a button
to close the garage door

Summer Solstice Quartet

(outdoor concert by the Borealis Quartet)

I

First violin, nerved up as a new mother,
strings, heart, eyes, tied to a baby's cry.
Second violin, thinking, *who can it be?*
Thoughts pulled left, then right.
Viola — some tender part, *hush,*
a kidney, or conscience.
All in the body of the cello,
cello bones, cello blood, cello cradle.

II

String quartets make us listen
for the heart's footsteps, but not the heart's footsteps
alone, oh no, not just that.
There's everything else, like time, trees, grief,
mail, mosquitoes, beggars, birds, time
again and again, as multitudinous as grass as
thick scores of notes, time rooting
into everything, growing into that heart.

III

The cello walks naked on the grass.
The viola remembers the moist chthonic
channels inside the living tree.
Second violin is crushed and scented on the hillside.
First violin, the wind, *benediction,* leaning
on grass, tree, hill, *benediction.* The trees lift
the baby's cries, bird song, over our heads,
just lift, not drop.

IV

June has come, a dear guest.
The trees clap their leaves along the path. The doorbell.
The birds are glad to hear such pleasant noise
for a change, mending machine tracks in their heads.
The birds' wings skitter more torn and airy
than the holy clouds. We notice
for the first time that we, too, are dressed in rags.
The door opens and the baby laughs.
We're in good company, finally.

Suburban Summer Ode

I – night

every few seconds air seeds the lungs
ploughs more dark into the clouds
gets more crusted with dog barks, cricket creaks, car rushes
trees tug-of-war wind mass and shadow
while blue TV light shivers at the windows
I thought I told my own story but as the dreams
blow in, they carry the dry rags
of a million mouths to my tongue
as it settles down in its moist nest

II – morning

a car door slams, an engine groans awake
clouds are cleaning the sky above the street
crisp shadows puzzle the driveway in black and white
magpies choose which eaves should carry walnuts
I wonder why the For Sale sign has suddenly appeared
when we're planting more hedges between us and the forest
all the windows are blinded by gold
two more cars drive away and none returns

III – afternoon

the dog attacks the glass as the girl delivers a flyer
the lawns are growing greener, how green can they get?
my neighbour has a pond and not one fish grows too big for it
cars, boats, RVs, trucks spill out of driveways and garages
I am keeping my flowers in pots as herons sometimes fly overhead
though I am not allowed to keep chickens I feed the birds
the ice cream trucks come less often now
and I don't miss them

IV – evening

the smell of charred meat vaults the fence
we talk about my friend's astronomy app
if you point the iphone down,
the Southern Cross appears on the screen
it's been beneath our feet all this time
the first star is like a stranger who comes to the door
the sunset so blurry we find ourselves wondering
what's happening out there?

Road Signs

I – Comfort

Don't you admire the white and green highway signs?
The ones that mark or tell you where the roadway goes?
Bannered above, they sort the traffic into lines
of cars going north, and some veering east, those ordering
arrows
gently saving us from hazard unless we panic
because we're going too fast, or we're lost. Even then they are
benevolent: they give us warning. If you are quick
the lanes may let you in. The signs that tell how far
are just as kindly. Often driving in this country
we travel endless miles of rocks or trees or grass.
We worry we're going nowhere, we missed a key
exit. For miles no signs, no buildings, just wilderness.
Then the white and green sign on the shoulder appears,
modestly
listing three towns and a logical lifeline of numbers as
promised.
Don't you trust these honest signs? Our society
at its best: rational as well as blessed.

II – Chaos

After the storm, your car on ice misses the exit.
The steering wheel moves, at first, in the right direction
but the tires are cut off, gone numb, some paralysis
has them. The highway signs drift by, watching, well-lit.
You violate each lane, sick at this defection.
What are signs now? Useless. Wilderness,
with its reader, weather, eradicates all texts.

Autumn Landscape

mountain pines rusting through
smudges of mist

maples, tea-coloured cellos
sumacs, small dragons

more milky mist
skim blue breast milk
mother of God of the fleecy mountains

earth rolling into winter
through the Milky Way's sharp teeth

Mission Ridge Riot

The ridge is a huge sand dune,
populated with deprived woods,
beetle-bitten trees,
invasive knapweed, crested wheat grass, baby's breath,
plastic pipe, beer cans, dog shit, human shit,
but native bunchgrass, too,
penstemon, dogbane, cactus, balsam root,
and more tough bush and flower.
But they're barely hanging on
to this dune
left high and dry ten thousand years ago
when the lake moved
four hundred feet below.

After rare Okanagan rain storms,
the dune goes on a drunken spree,
slashing gouges into already eroded slopes,
stuffing ditches with loose trash,
exposing pines to be true redheads by yanking
soil off their rosy roots,
looting paths of their directions.
And when the dune hits suburban streets,
backyards, sidewalks —
it's wet sand all over the place.

But the mess is tidied up immediately.
We'll have no little rogue beaches popping up
in this neighbourhood,
devaluing the million-dollar frontage by the lake.
The dune slinks back to its hill
and its dependants,
once again letting go of the dream, but
glad it got to drag us all
a little bit down.

Water into Wine

Miracula! The beginning of the signs!
That summer night in Galilee, all nature stood outside
and watched the party flood the evening courtyards,
and soaking dancers collapse onto cushions,
with stars half-lost in billows of smoke
from burning cedar and roasting meat.
The whole village of Cana was there
(this was before the first bad heat wave)
even the bride's second cousin, what's her name?,
the annoying one, with her holier-than-thou pickle-face,
the one who stood by the BBQ slopping up the hummus
talking about how she didn't eat dead lambs,
or arguing with anyone who'd listen about the waste
of putting wine in new wineskins, "why not recycle the old?"
She was a prune and a pest.
Who wants to talk about dryland salinity
and declining river systems at a wedding?
(This was before the seas started shrinking.)
She was sniffing around the rain barrels
when the servants discovered the wine
was almost gone! What a scandal
it could have been! The wedding of the year!
But the Preacher's mother — the gossips say
she's sweet on the Master of the Feast —
dragged her poor Son over. He seemed reluctant at first.
He was heard to say,
  "Woman, do we know what we are doing?"
That silly cousin saw what was happening;
she'd heard the rumours about Him.
"Don't," she lunged at Him, "We need the water."
Too bad she touched Him as His hand reached the lip
of the water pots. My God!

The sheer quantity of that merlot!
And we've tasted nothing like it since.
It was like drinking melted silk.
Lord, the feast was talked about for months!
The bride stained in hock from head to ruby toe,
the groom slung to the marriage bed
in a carpet where the woven vines
and henna blooms were blotted black with sack,
and the servants laid their sozzled bodies in the hyssop
so, for days, minty musk mingled with
the smell of scorch and vomit.
We have torn up all our orchards and planted vineyards!
The cousin?
Oh, her arm being withered to the bone
and her skin having lost all sense,
she lives among the lepers in the dust,
begging for her daily bread and water,
a tough life anytime, but especially now
that we're living through this drought.

Water Main

done by the developer down the road
done by breaking some buried pipe
my house is thirsty terribly
thirsty   the toilet gulps a last greedy
the taps cough up a
the bathtub is chewing its
shingles lick lick mucky gutters and I sit
alone at a table with one small bottle of

living on a ship teetering on scaffolds of pipes and drains
shipwrecked in a house helpless
as a sewage-filled whale on a beach
whose giant liver and heart slowly sink into gravel
whose own ribs skewer it from the inside
who becomes a shish-kebab on its own bones
barbecuing in the sun

why can no one ever haul a whale off a beach
why do we think we're gods with our tankers and our bathrooms
when we can't even haul a whale off a beach to save our lives
or find a drop of whatever
to wash our hands
when a pipe's been done in
by a developer down the road
done in by burying
          our naked need
in a ditch
done in
and done

Windfall

I

everything the wind shakes out of trees,
all that is loose, ripe, caught
and dead:
wandering leaves, birds' nests,
pine cones and golden needles,
children with broken arms,
a robin's egg in spring,
snow bombs in winter,
lynched men with bits of sky attached,
cracked branches, bloody feathers
the oldest apples on the earth

II

little rows of lemons
drop into place, a doll's mechanical eyes
surprised
when the casino collapses
and metal entrails of machines
demolish
the floor

III

the wind fell, tripped
over a mountain
skidded through pear trees
smashed into trunks so
fruit landed everywhere

now the fallen wind
is sprawled, hair
tangled in unmown grass
face planted
in the mud the pears
bruised and leaking
beneath its cheek

IV

It's a windfall,
not a calm fall, not a fall
for long walks in Indian summer.
This fall the wind
has bought the whole season,
sells its shares on October's streets.
It speculates with razors and deeds,
perfects an aggressive sales pitch,
grabs you by the collar with an icy fist
when you trespass on its beach.
It's a windfall, a conspiracy
between wealth and weather,
with the real estate agents and city councillors
pushing you around,
knocking you down
if you complain of their invasion,
their overblown returns.

V

The cold came
so early
the leaves had no time
to fall.
They stayed on
the trees

for months
till a winter storm
plucked them off
every grey-skinned branch
and threw
the crackling litter
down.
Brittle leaves blew
back and forth across
the crusty snow,
rattling and rustling.
The wind tossed the orchard
like a toy.
The racket!

VI

the snow so deep in the woods
hunger pulls the deer down
the mountain

the animal bellies are ploughs
they furrow their way through
the night
to dormant orchards

with their cloven hooves
they till the snow
rake matted weed and eat

the fruit, their eyes the colour
of sticky brown rot

Landing

Tear it up, tear it up. I am ashamed of my own handwriting, afraid of the emptiness of a page of words, the orderly pad of paper. My hand is always busy.

Is there no place to rest my foot? The word "settler" is mine but I stare at it with no understanding.

I see Jeannette across the room. She is speaking.

I write down a word I cannot say.

I put down the pen and the book. Shut my eyes. Link my hands in my lap. Fingers braid together. Empty palms.

If I can hear her voice

If I can hear the chickadee

If I can hear the world I am in

well, it may take this long

a tree's life

but I wrote it down once and I hear Jeannette speaking,

tmxʷulaxʷ

– III –

Woodhaven:
A Crisis of Place

Striped Coralroot, Cougar

in the bottom of a desert valley
        in a dark wood
troubled, I walked

and stumbled upon a creature
        orchid-weird and bloody-clawed:
a botanical jaguar

chopped by its leafless fang
        its striped snarl,   I turned,
fled, clumsy, dumb-thoughted,

pursued by that soul empurpled
        charnelled,   foaming
its wild way through dark woods

its white foot churning alive the rot
        glimpsed once,   eyelash tattooed
this new Beatrice

a sight to take me down
        unplait me, pick me open, and maybe
twist me into one
                wrung root

Off the Path, in the Dark Woods

having a crisis of place

in the intersection of four bioclimactic zones. Which way to
go? Where is my guide?

Everything is jointed, not listed. Everything is antler, not
border.

Geography takes its sweet time. The long dying and drying of
the cottonwood zone knits into

the needle gristle of the Douglas fir zone, which stitches in
and out of the long hem of

the ponderosa pine zone as it throws itself down over years,
over decades, down the cliffside in a swoon of butterfly skirt
and cactus, right into

the braided arms of the western red cedar zone, brooding in
its dark melancholy, studying its drought. O Byronic cedars
weeping moisture into the air, pressing curly moss onto the
brow of

the cottonwood zone. Look at geography and time twin, brail,
and trellis another moment, another failure, another stone
into place, in

the intersection of four bioclimactic zones, having a crisis of
place.

Joan Burbridge: A Guide

dear spirit, find me, haul

me through the park, your book,   open
the leaves,
        lantern the needle-incandescent paths,
take my tongue to task, pin

me in my tracks, slow me into

the where
        of my ears and feet

      take me in
           to this place   step
           by planting step,
               with crisis clear

                  with eyes open

Guide's Book: Wild Flowers of the Southern Interior of British Columbia

A field guide with 335 species of flowering plants and a comprehensive listing of their many names — English, local, Latin, nostalgic, all unhooked from their Nsyilxcen names. Stamp-sized faded photos, dark woods lurking behind many, others with sun overexposing the page. *Heal-all, duck potato, naked broomrape.* This "beautiful and useful book will be a welcome addition to the library [knapsack, window sill] of any naturalist [dog-walker, flower-liker, wilderness tourist, developer-fighter, nature-dilettante]." Like the flower painters of yore, it's a woman isn't it? *Lapland cassiope, spotted kirtle-pink, partridge foot, puccoon.* Small enough to fit in a bag with a bottle of water and a handful of almonds. Coded in petal colour. Its cover pink as *spreading dogbane, bitterroot, penstemon,* new favourite flowers of the spring. Can anyone ever have called knapweed *star thistle*? No indigenous name for that zombie. No ghost word haunting that one.

Enter Here

Is the water lower
in the creek this year? Are bees
and blossoms fewer? I take the path,
follow the spirit, her field guide
in hand. I'm sad, yet feeling joy.
The flowers wash, then dry my eyes.
The body jumps its categories.
I'm on a journey that backtracks
over pages, down paths, finds
then forgets streams and glimpses. Caught
in a lasso of green and white and yellow,
the path loops in smaller circles,
the book's a comedy, but not a story.
I learn the multiple names of flowers —
language-y garlands to hang in my brain.

Braiding

– circle one

An emptiness that has the trick
of substance as all parking lots do.
Here, the shades of long-dead city councillors,
developers, real estate agents, contractors
beneath our feet plead innocence.
Why shouldn't they do deals in the dark?
Why shouldn't land worth $75,000
in May, be worth $125,000
in June? Unwearied spirits, still the eternal
machinations going on,
eating away at borders, wasting
water and killing trees,
as we hide in the hot houses
they've built us, glowing like forges,
saying we didn't know, it's what
we believed, this gas and oil keeping
us just right until judgement day
as the shades in the parking lot
try to crawl out of the gravel,
want to sink their teeth into
asphalt-their-meat, tongues
going gooey, soft and stalled.

thread

A dry, cold spring. Worried,
helpless, snow pack only half
its depth, I stumble through

this rusting fenced-in sea of flowers:
sunflower banks of balsam root,
frothy false Solomon's seal,
Saskatoon blooms that swell then
roll out berries, Oregon grape
bubbling yellow, hairbrain dashes
of fleabane, light slaps of wild roses,
creamy green jellyfishing
elderberry, slow motion spray
of cottonwood seed whitecapping
the ground. And all the plants I don't know,
the immersing, green, anonymous main.
Even the air's a liquid, tall trees
stirring it round; the flowers float
and nod over the sloshing earth,
pine pollen salting every
inch, all the rocking stones
and masting trunks. Lost, I'm wading,
sinking into the height and depth
of the sensuous world, the bone-sewn,
name-spattered, leaf-smothered,
pollen-rubbed, bark-trenched,
birdsong-battered, fur-mottled,
branch-cracking, petal-lit,
vertical park. Away, outside
the gate, among the great wounds
of suburbs and roads, history hurricanes,
children are struck by malls and screens,
our homes hawsered by wires and cement.
In the park, drought and disease drop
great trees, one at a time.

– circle two

animals pick around our litter

the bear shoulders
the rattle of metal flume

the deer teaches twin fawns to side-
    step the rusty cans
        of the settlers' midden

my cells shed into the wind

    I am a dissolving bag of scent

animals avoid my body's wake
        its smell of chemical, plastic, machine,
        and meat

     thread

the trees are all
                   all gesture, all power
all secret nest holes
        and wind-cracked limbs

their needles and leaves
    fold owl calls into
        evening air
air full of the trees' thinking

they are thinking through deep problems,
        thinking through hard earth and stone,

laying down the dark laws
    of humus

and, mostly, staying,

    for staying,
        staying and thinking,
            is their business

– circle three

in the evening, twenty-three vultures
    write graffiti in the sky
        they're Banksy
it's dogpatch up there
        they're rolling barbed wire into the sky

and down below
    strung along the foot of the clifted slope
are rusted fences
    our garbage-y fangs lying in ditches
    down here where we eat and sleep in
        our trash

to the vultures, we're jokes
    they're writing in the weather

        what do we hear?
strange jangly music at the fair

DDT was banned in the 1970s. Woodhaven was established in 1973 after a community battle with developers. The surrounding orchards and backyards are full of robins eating DDT-saturated earthworms, even after forty years. The regions in robins' brains responsible for singing and mating shrink when exposed to high levels of DDT (Iwaniuk et al 2006). DDE levels (a breakdown product of the insecticide, DDT) are still 100 parts per million in birds' eggs from orchard sites. This is ten times higher than in non-orchard areas of the Okanagan valley (Elliott *et al.* 1994). Peregrine falcons can breed successfully only if they feed primarily on mourning doves which do not feed in orchards. Feeding on as little as 10 percent of other species such as starlings, robins, gulls and magpies produces DDE concentrations in peregrine eggs greater than the danger threshold. Based on the level of DDE contamination of prey, it seems unlikely that peregrine falcons can breed successfully throughout most of the Okanagan Valley of British Columbia (Elliott et. al 2004).

thread

I moved next door to Woodhaven Nature Conservancy. I knew nothing about it or what it conserved. My house is built on a former peach orchard. Hawks and vultures circle above. At my bird feeder: mourning doves, quail, sparrows, chickadees, juncos, finches, robins. A hawk sweeps into the homely pecking scene. It slowly tears apart a quail on the roof of my garden shed, shredding muscle, tendons, feathers.

– circle five

Ringed round the park, outside the fence,
is the woeful world, the cement basements
stamped into the earth, stone patios strangling
unnaturally blue pools, wooden decks
toxified and painted, new houses off-gassing,
gravel pits with rotten knapweed teeth.

It is the woeful world, the burnt forests
on the hills with branches sizzled off,
their pointed trunks like ugly black hairs
you should pluck. Fireweed empurples
the slope like giant bruises.
The charcoal trunks, their grave-baked limbs.

Even in the park, even with my guide,
even walking beneath the benedicting boughs
of cedar, I think of suicidal drought and want.
The sweet and scented path. The guidebook.
What we think we're doing with parks and preserves.
Some conscience set aside, some excuse.

– circle six

the chain-link fence around
the park is bejewelled with berries,
                                around
the entire border, chokers of rose hips
hoards of maggot-white snowberries,
    chains of chokecherry necklaces
                        all born again in huge splats
of bear scat on the paths, peppered
with skin and pit   it's hot in here

                    four people
fled in terror this week as the bear
shouldered in for a good
nosh
        it's a happy demon-bear,
pronging and pitchforking
the shrubby limbs, stripping their purses
of seedy treasure
                    not even the ants
in their millions biting ankles and legs
        guard the park
with such verve
                        watch out walkers,
the bear wears this fence like a ring.

            thread

look at the fence in front of you,
your skin, too, sieves hot and cold
your skin is your chain link fence

– *circle seven*

It's a desert. The snow in the hills
doesn't come down much anymore.

White people cannot live here without
ice and air conditioners and water
bombers.

Ash and cinders fall like snow.
Smoke snowplows the sun.

Bulldozer heat clubs down
forests, eats canyons, fills
the air with its terrible stench.

Airplanes rise dripping out
of the lake, water bellied,
wing tips on fire.

The park is a small green panic,
It's a green forest heart, fibrillating,
then still

as the cigarette drops
its pitchfork sparks
on the path.

      thread

red flesh of ponderosa pine,
long back curving into the ground,
splitting, that thick case of bark opening,
releasing its wooden memories of wind

once a cave for owls, now a trough
for crawling animals and leafy beddings,
smooth bone of cottonwood, softened
from the inside, having drunk itself rotten

western red cedar, pumpkin-coloured
straw on the forest floor, its shredded
mat undoing itself, unbraiding for decades
then rebraiding with fungi, invertebrates

all these giant bodies call as I pass by
"what's happening up there?"
creating earth, after centuries
of making air

– circle figure-eighting

The trails in the park loop around inside a fence; they are not a journey. The paths braid your feet into soil, directions, twigs, stories. Sometimes you have to take a path you have walked before.

the flume trail — the park in the past

When we are children, we are immersed in sensation. We feel every rich moment of our long, thing-filled days, and everything that happens to us, everything that we eat, touch, or see, is astonishing. But when we get to ten, or eleven, or twelve years old (when did it happen to you?) consciousness erupts in our bodies, its massive branches blooming in our heads. The self begins its great blotting, prickling invasion, so intense, so mushrooming, many cannot bear it, so try to crush it, smother it, kill it, push it down with drugs, or drink, or fantasies, or reading, or video games, or manias, or busy little gangs of thugs or friends, anything to distract us from the rampant, exploding awareness and its terrible hunger for meanings. No one teaches us how to live with this new thing in us. No one helps us know what it is.

the main trail — the park in the present

We advise you to come to the woods. Sit down and look at a large tree moving in a breeze. Think of each tree as a mirror to one of your thoughts. The tens of thousands of leaves twist and flip, the branches stir and bend, the roots and filaments crack through dirt and rock beneath you in darkness. Each leaf, each filament rubs and strokes the nerves knotted in your brain. All around you are your other thoughts. Each thought, like each tree, is being cooled and rubbed and thumbed open. Learn the ecology of your brain. Air out each wiry worry, each sticky obsession. As Rilke says, so often we don't notice or even care that we are alive. Be dazzled by the beauty of your heartbeat, marvel at the self as it becomes shy when you are perfectly alone. Sit on Joan's bench for a time and be with yourself as you are.

the border — the park in the future

Million dollar mansions are being built on the sand dunes above the park. Teetering above the cliff edges are trembling swimming pools of chemicals. Someone above has emptied a chlorinated pool down the cliff, into the park. Its gravelly channel is gouged into ugly runnels down the slope. I am in the long history of the literate but memory is face down, its back carved open. There is no terror here. I feel no terror. Snow begins to fall.

– circle nine

it's a forest gut-punched with yellow
cartoon gold pours out its open mouth
temperate climates breed greed
conquistadors rifle through closets of yellow mail
drawers of rattling chains and straps
what to wear to the massacre?
the leaves squeeze into yellow wing suits
drop and dive at buckled helmets,
it's getting late, hurry, hurry
march along the jangling paths strewn with corpses
Oregon grape snaps at spurs like feral dogs
everything between head and heel is Midas-ing
and on the tip of the sword, a bubble of rosehip

(more numerous than fireflies, within the flame
of each leaf is a spirit, enfolded in what burns it)

it's the cult of the cloves' annual dance
now the lemon cocktail bites the lips
eyes tango from sequined shrub to stripping tree
the El Dorado dance floor is breaking up
beneath boots and axe of breastplate
the glorious golden cleavage heaves
with the brain's last sigh of "oh yes"
before November's gun metal wind cracks down

– circle, in a drain

There is water. And there isn't water. Sometimes the cotton-
woods wade and rot happily in the stream. Sometimes the
cedars with their great lyred throats thirst. Houses all around
the park have flooded basements. This was a riparian zone.
Creeks weave and sponge all around the park and under the
new houses. Solution: shut off the water. The park has a fence
around it and there are signs — nature conservancy. It'll be
safe. Turn off the tap. Shut the sluice gates. It'll be safe.
A pretty creek, big trees. They'll survive. Turn off the water,
stop it from running into our houses and under the roots.
Change everything, just like that! Creek, street, mountain,
plant, bird. We own all the gravity, too, as we own rattlesnake
dens, cedars, water, language. The creek's long string, down
the waterfall, through the canyon, woolly and sweet, and soon
spiralled into a sewer's knot.

Moon Circle

full winter moon
                moon
                    moon

      massive moon hands part cedar curtains
      raccoon thieves drag their moon-ring sacks behind

          the glittering! the searchlights!
          Gordon Road sirens and engines!
          the wood burgled clean by the switchblade moon

owls roll moon in their beaks like dice
and strip the mice of their furry fortunes

          who's calling to the bones inside you?
          your buried moon joints, your slippery moon sockets

          look with your moon ball eyes
          with their hollow black centres

who will the moon ransack next?
you?   will it be
you?

Guide's Last Words

Protect This Place

— Be uncertain in the woods. What do you really know?

— Ignore the asphalt sermons you hear every day.

— Cain in the moon. Coyote in the moon. You choose.

— Nature does not repent making bears or cougars.

— Be polite in the forest. It is not a mountain or a lake.

— All around you is the massive implementation of
roots and cells.

— Remember: Nature has also imagined You.

— And what's inside you.

— Ask yourself, ask the rattlesnake: could you stay?

ACKNOWLEDGEMENTS

—

Some of these poems or versions of them have been published in the chapbook *Okanagan Galilee* (Alfred Gustav Press), in *Entanglements: New Ecopoetry* (Two Ravens Press (UK)), and in the journals *Dandelion*, *CV2*, *The Goose*, *Okanagan Arts*, *The National Post Online*, as well as the publications of the Woodhaven Eco Art Project in Kelowna BC.

I would like to thank Sylvie Desjardins who invited me to participate in the Behr's hairstreak research project and the creative writing workshop at the Banff International Research Station for Mathematical Innovation and Discovery. I am grateful to Lori Mairs who did so much to inspire the Woodhaven poems, including allowing me access, in many ways, to the park and its living beings, its history, and its special places. I would like to thank Tia Mclennan, Shed Simas, Lori Mairs, and Denise Kenney who through their own art contributed to the development of the Woodhaven poems. The Woodhaven poems came out of a year-long eco art project funded by the Hampton Fund of UBC, and I would like to thank the fund and the many people at UBC's Okanagan campus who supported this project. I would like to thank my many students over the years who invited me to participate in their annual World Water Day Poetry slam, an event that inspired a few of the poems in this book. I am grateful to the naturalists and scientists who let me accompany them on walks and attend talks, particularly Don Gayton, the Master of Grass. I would like to thank Jeannette Armstrong who allowed me to attend her UBC course on Okanagan perspectives, a truly transformative experience. I must acknowledge the wealth of information found in various books and guides, particularly Joan

Burbridge's *Wildflowers of the Southern Interior of British Columbia and Adjacent Parts of Washington, Idaho and Montana;* Parish, Coupe and Lloyd's *Plants of the Southern Interior;* the *Kaufman Focus Guide to Butterflies of North America;* and countless bird identification books which often have such poetic passages. The italicized stanza in "Circle Nine" is from Dante's *Inferno,* Canto 26, taken loosely from Robert Pinsky's translation. I am deeply grateful for my creative writing colleagues at UBC's Okanagan campus, Sharon Thesen, Michael V. Smith, Anne Fleming, and Adam Lewis Schroeder, who are brilliant, supportive, witty, generous, and always a dream team. Most of all, I am grateful to Dave Murray for his loving support, for our daily walks, and for his generous tolerance of all the time I spend at my desk or in my office.

I would like to acknowledge the Syilx people of the Okanagan First Nations whose rights and title to their traditional territory, which includes the Okanagan valley, are unceded and untreatied, as is so much land in British Columbia.

ABOUT THE AUTHOR

—

Nancy Holmes has published four collections of poetry, most recently *Mandorla* (Ronsdale Press, 2005). Her other books are *The Adultery Poems* (Ronsdale, 2002), *Down to the Golden Chersonese: Victorian Lady Travellers* (Sono Nis, 1991), and *Valancy and the New World* (Kalamalka Press, 1988). She is also the editor of *Open Wide a Wilderness: Canadian Nature Poems* (Wilfrid Laurier University Press, 2009). For twenty years, she has lived in the Okanagan Valley of British Columbia where she teaches Creative Writing at the Okanagan campus of the University of British Columbia and organizes eco art projects throughout the valley. She lives in Kelowna, B.C.

RECYCLED
Paper made from
recycled material
FSC® C103567
www.fsc.org

Marquis Book Printing Inc.

Québec, Canada
2012

Printed on Silva Enviro 100% post-consumer EcoLogo certified paper,
processed chlorine free and manufactured using biogas energy.